YOU CHOOSE
BOOKS

HERCULES
AND HIS 12 LABORS

AN INTERACTIVE MYTHOLOGICAL ADVENTURE

by Anika Fajardo
illustrated by Nadine Takvorian

Consultant: Dr. Laurel Bowman
Department of Greek and Roman Studies
University of Victoria
Victoria, BC, Canada

CAPSTONE PRESS
a capstone imprint

You Choose Books are published by Capstone Press,
1710 Roe Crest Drive, North Mankato, Minnesota 56003
www.capstonepub.com

Library of Congress Cataloging-in-Publication Data
Cataloging-in-Publication Data is on file with the Library of Congress.
978-1-4914-8111-0 (hardcover)
978-1-4914-8116-5 (paperback)
978-1-4914-8120-2 (eBook PDF)

Editorial Credits
Michelle Hasselius, editor, Russell Griesmer, designer; Wanda Winch,
media researcher, Kathy McColley, production specialist

Image Credits
Shutterstock: Alex Novikov, paper scroll, Eky Studio, old stone wall,
reyhan, piece of stone, Samira Dragonfly, Baroque frame, Tymokno Galyna,
Greek columns, Zvonimir Atletic, 102

Table of Contents

About Your Adventure

YOU are the demi-god, Hercules. You must complete 12 tasks in 12 years to earn forgiveness for crimes you committed against your family. These tasks will put you face-to-face with dangerous monsters, deadly warriors, and godly enemies. Will you complete your tasks, or die trying?

Chapter One sets the scene. Then you choose which path to take. Follow the directions at the bottom of each page. The choices you make determine what happens next. After you finish your path, go back and read the others for more adventures.

YOU CHOOSE the path you take through this mythical adventure.

Becoming a Hero

Life in 400 B.C. is difficult for people in Greece. There are many deadly battles between people in different lands. Wars are common, and dangerous beasts roam the lands. Floods and droughts kill crops. Kings and rulers change as frequently as the seasons. To help make sense of the world around them, the people turn to gods and goddesses for guidance, protection, and comfort.

Your father, Zeus, is one of the gods the Greeks worship. Zeus is king of all the Greek gods and goddesses that reign over Mount Olympus. You are the mighty hero Hercules.

Turn the page.

But you are only half-god. Your mother is a mortal woman named Alcmene. Your very existence has made you a deadly enemy. Zeus' wife, the goddess Hera, is jealous of her husband's love for your mother. And this jealousy has made her angry with you too.

Hera has tried to kill you before. When you were a baby, Hera put two poisonous serpents into your crib. But you were not afraid of the serpents' red eyes and sharp fangs. Instead you easily strangled the snakes to death with your bare hands.

As you grew, you learned how to use a sword and drive a chariot. The god Apollo taught you how to use a bow and arrow. Now that you are a man, you are taller, stronger, and braver than any other. You are clearly the son of a god.

When Hera sees how strong and skilled you have become, she devises a plan to destroy you once and for all. One night Hera causes you to fall into a confused, violent rage. In the chaos, you fail to recognize those around you. Your beloved wife, Megara, and your children are killed as a result.

Once you come to your senses, you realize what you have done. In your agony, you pray to Apollo for guidance. The god tells you to serve King Eurystheus of Mycenae for 12 years as punishment for killing your family. The king has a reputation of being cruel. It will not be an easy time. But by serving the king, your crime will be forgiven.

Turn the page.

But Hera is not finished with you yet. She convinces King Eurystheus to challenge you to 12 impossible tasks that no mortal man could survive. But there is some good news.

"If you complete these 12 labors," King Eurystheus promises you, "you will gain both forgiveness from the gods and your immortality. Instead of dying, you will live among the gods at Mount Olympus forever."

You may be the strongest man in the world, and the prize is right. But you are still half-human. How can you possibly complete these impossible labors?

But in the end, you have no choice. You must accept King Eurystheus' challenge. You will earn both forgiveness and immortality. Where do you begin?

To attempt the first four labors and track the vicious Nemean Lion,
turn to page 13.

To start your labors by facing the stables of King Augeas,
turn to page 41.

To battle the Amazon queen and complete the rest of the labors,
turn to page 71.

CHAPTER 2

The Nemean Lion

You arrive at the palace in Mycenae and await instructions from King Eurystheus.

"Your first task," King Eurystheus says in a bold voice, "is to fetch me the hide of the Nemean Lion."

After a short journey, you arrive in Nemea with your sharp dagger, sword, and heavy club. You find that the lion has ravaged the countryside. The people are terrified out of their wits. They tell you of a horrible creature with a hide that no spear can pierce.

Turn the page.

One of the townspeople, an old man in ragged clothes, shakes his head. "You will certainly die trying."

You feel anger rise in your chest. You know you are the strongest man in the world, and you are not afraid. You'll show him! You set out to track the lion. It doesn't take long before you find it roaming the dry hills, searching for any living creature to have for lunch. As an expert hunter, you slowly approach the lion. Its golden mane glistens in the sunlight. You creep closer, gripping your weapons. Just then the lion raises its head. It has caught your scent. The beast leaps toward you, its claws outstretched. How will you protect yourself from this creature?

To battle the lion with a sword and dagger,
go to page 15.

To battle the lion with a club,
turn to page 17.

You grab your sword with your right hand. You clutch your dagger in your left. Armed with these two blades, you are certain you will be able to defeat the Nemean Lion. But the lion is too quick for you. Even before you have a chance to strike, it sinks its sharp teeth into your forearm.

You back up and attack from the side. Your dagger meets the hide of the beast, but it cannot pierce it. The beast roars as if it has been tickled. It spins around and snaps the blade in half.

Turn the page.

Your blood boils with anger and frustration. You shout at the deadly beast and rush toward it with your sword flashing in the sunlight. But the sword bounces off the lion's sleek coat.

The lion leaps at you, knocking you to the ground. You feel a heavy weight on your chest. The last thing you hear before you die is the growl of the terrible Nemean Lion.

THE END

To follow another path, turn to page 11.

To learn more about Hercules, turn to page 103.

No spear can pierce the lion. So you are thankful you have brought your club. You grasp the heavy wood in your right hand. With your left, you make a strong fist. As the lion leaps toward you, you strike. You hit the lion with all your might. The lion backs away before charging you again. You swing each time it charges. Finally the deadly beast falls lifeless to the dirt. Using the beast's own razor-sharp claws, you skin the lion. You drape the hide over you like a cape.

With the hide on your back, you return to Mycenae. King Eurystheus greets you as you enter the palace. His mouth drops open in shock when he sees you wearing the lion's hide.

"As commanded," you say, "I have the hide of the Nemean Lion."

Turn the page.

"V … v … very well," King Eurystheus stammers. His eyes are wide in disbelief. "Your next task is to kill the Hydra in Lerna."

The Hydra is a giant, deadly snake creature with nine heads. It will be hard to kill. But you agree. You shoulder your club and sword.

"And when you return, Hercules, you are forbidden from entering my palace," King Eurystheus says, looking around anxiously at his servants. "From now on, you will get your instructions from my servant at the gate."

Still wearing the lion's hide, you travel to Lerna. Your nephew Iolaus joins you, eager to watch his uncle battle dangerous creatures. In the marshy lowland near the city, you find the Hydra. The Hydra's heads swarm and squirm like a pile of worms, each mouth lined with dagger-shaped teeth.

Sword in hand, you easily slice off one of the Hydra's heads. But almost as soon as the head falls to the ground, another grows in its place. You begin slashing at the beast. But every time you cut off a head, a new one grows. Each new head tries to kill you with its sharp teeth.

As you work at killing the beast, dusk falls. It is becoming more difficult to see the swarming heads.

"Uncle!" shouts Iolaus. "Let me help you!" You turn to see your nephew holding a lighted torch. The torch's light shines on the Hydra's terrible teeth.

To tell Iolaus to use his torch to fight the Hydra, turn to page 21.

To continue fighting the Hydra alone, turn to page 27.

As another one of the Hydra's heads falls to the ground, an idea comes to you. "Come here with that torch, Iolaus," you say. "But be careful."

Iolaus approaches the Hydra as you cut off another head. The head tumbles to the ground, its mouth still screaming.

"Now use the burning torch to close off the wound on this beast's neck," you tell your nephew. As he places the flame onto the creature's neck, the melted flesh of the serpent's neck sizzles. No new head grows back. You cut off another head, and Iolaus once again seals off the wound. Swiftly you and Iolaus work to destroy each of the beast's heads. When at last you cut off the final head, the Hydra falls to the ground, dead.

Turn the page.

"I couldn't have done it without you, Iolaus," you say. "Now I must return to Mycenae for my next labor."

When you arrive in Mycenae, you shout, "Tell King Eurystheus that I have killed the Hydra!"

The king's servant delivers the message to Eurystheus. But when the servant returns, he tells you, "The king says this labor will not count. You did it with the help of your nephew."

"What?" you say. "Let me speak to him!"

The servant says, "You are not allowed to enter the king's palace. He is hiding in a large bronze urn."

"He must be very afraid of me," you say, laughing. "Very well. What new task has he given to me?"

"This time you are to bring back the Cerynean stag," the servant says. "You must return within one year."

You set off for Mount Keryneia, the area where the stag is known to roam. When you arrive, the people who live in the foothills of Mount Keryneia tell you more about the Cerynean stag.

"It is the most beautiful deer that ever lived!" says a young man. "And the fastest."

"You'll know it by its golden hooves and golden horns," says a woman with a baby on her hip.

Just as you are about to thank the villagers, the young man adds, "You know, of course, that the Cerynean stag is Artemis' favorite creature ... right?"

Turn the page.

You stop in your tracks. Artemis is the goddess of wild animals. She loves all living things and believes in protecting the young and beautiful. And Artemis is quick to kill anyone who upsets her. Her bow and arrow are swift, and she never misses.

"Artemis is not my master. King Eurystheus has decided my task," you say, holding tight to your bow. "I must find the stag."

You head into the hills to search for the animal. Before long, you see a flash of gold. The stag's golden horns catch the sunlight. You begin the chase. You continue running after the stag until all the light is gone from the sky. In the morning you awake only to chase the stag again. But the deer is always just beyond your reach.

Turn the page.

Several weeks pass. You are exhausted and annoyed. You curse both King Eurystheus and Artemis. Just as you have run out of patience, you see the animal once again. It stands near a thicket of juniper bushes.

To chase after the stag,
turn to page 29.

To end the chase and kill the stag,
turn to page 33.

"Stay away, Iolaus!" you shout as one of the Hydra's heads comes dangerously close to your nephew.

"But I want to help," he says.

"You are just a boy," you tell him. Iolaus is strong but no match for the Hydra. "Keep back so you aren't hurt."

You continue cutting and slicing at the monster. You swing your sword with great skill and accuracy. Over and over you cut off the beast's heads. But try as you might, a new head always grows back almost as quickly as you slice it off.

"Uncle?" you hear your nephew call again.

"What?" you growl. You are angry now. You are covered in sweat and blood and dirt. Your sword is coated in the muck of the Hydra.

Turn the page.

"Uncle, I don't think this beast will die," Iolaus says. He holds the torch closer to the monster so you can get a better look. Just then, the Hydra turns to Iolaus and the torch. One of its heads lunges toward him.

"Look out!" you shout. You push Iolaus out of the way in the nick of time. But you are not so lucky. The Hydra's poisonous teeth sink into your neck. It feels like hundreds of sharp knives cutting into you. You collapse to the ground and die.

THE END

To follow another path, turn to page 11.

To learn more about Hercules, turn to page 103.

Just then a blur of white and gold can be seen across the valley. There it is: The Cerynean stag. You take off running again, but the stag is always just out of reach. As you continue to chase it, you realize its pace has slowed. That's when you decide how you'll catch the stag. You will tire it out.

You take a deep breath and chase after the animal again. Eleven long months pass. You are exhausted and frustrated but still no closer to catching the stag. But you never raise your bow. You know it would do no good to anger Artemis. It is best to keep all the gods on your side.

At long last your patience pays off. On a cool evening just as the sun sets, the deer slows and staggers. Then it finally collapses with exhaustion. You are also exhausted. But your quest is not over yet.

Turn the page.

You gently pick up the beautiful creature and carry it back to Mycenae.

"Here I am," you tell the king's messenger when you arrive. "Tell Eurystheus I've brought the stag."

The king's messenger leads you to a fenced-in area. "Let it go," he tells you. "King Eurystheus wants the stag to run in his pastures."

"I hope it runs away," you mutter under your breath. But you release the stag.

After the stag has run off, the messenger turns to you. "Your next labor," he says, "is to go to Arcadia. Capture the Erymanthian boar. Then you must bring it back here alive."

When you arrive in Arcadia, you are told that the boar has been frightening children, killing men, and leaving destruction in its path. The people of Arcadia tell you that you will find the beast on Mount Erymanthus.

"It will be easy to track the boar in the snow," says one of the men in town.

The climb to Mount Erymanthus is rocky. As you journey higher, the air feels cold and sharp. Snow that doesn't melt, even in summer, is packed in hard frozen drifts.

Just as you reach the summit, you hear snorting and stomping. A towering creature appears from behind a snow-covered boulder.

Turn the page.

The Erymanthian boar is bigger than you imagined. Its large, yellowed tusks are stained with blood. Saliva drips from its mouth. The boar lowers its head to attack, and you brace yourself for a battle with the beast. But perhaps you could run, and the boar will tire itself. It worked with the stag. It may work again.

To run away from the boar,
turn to page 36.

To face the boar,
turn to page 38.

You cannot run any farther. You know Artemis loves wild creatures, but there seems like no way to capture the stag alive. You hope Artemis will understand. You take aim with your bow and arrow.

As you let your arrow loose, the stag bolts again, away from danger. Your arrow bounces off a tree, doing no harm. The stag, spooked, darts through the underbrush. You follow, determined now.

The stag bounds into open pastureland. You set another arrow into the bow. You have a clear shot now. You breathe deeply, take careful aim, and shoot. You've done it this time. The stag rises for an instant, then falls to the ground, dead.

Turn the page.

"Hercules, what have you done?" you hear a mighty voice boom behind you. You turn and see the goddess Artemis. Her eyes glint with anger. In her bow is a silver arrow.

"Not even Zeus will protect you now," she says as she aims her bow at your heart. Her arrow kills you instantly.

THE END

To follow another path, turn to page 11.

To learn more about Hercules, turn to page 103.

You begin sprinting down the mountain. You can hear the snorting of the boar behind you, and feel its huge hooves hammering the ground as it runs. Running downhill is tough, and the hard snow makes it even more difficult. Your feet sting in the cold snow. Your only hope is that the boar is getting tired too.

All of a sudden, you slip on a piece of ice and fall. The ice cuts your hands and knees as you catch yourself. You scramble to get up again, but it takes you a moment longer to get back on your feet. When you turn to look back, the boar has almost reached you.

You turn to run, but you already feel hot breath at your back. The boar has caught up with you despite your speed. It rams its head into your legs, sending you tumbling onto the snow. It pins you to the ground, and you know there is no hope. The Erymanthian boar's sharp tusks rip into your flesh.

THE END

To follow another path, turn to page 11.

To learn more about Hercules, turn to page 103.

The boar charges, and you grab its huge neck in your arms. You flip the deadly beast onto its back, careful to avoid its sharp tusks. But the boar will not give up that easily. It struggles to its feet, jerking you to the ground. Sharp hooves angrily paw the snow before the boar lunges toward you again.

But you are quicker and stronger than the boar. You leap to your feet. This time you manage to grab the boar's tusks and wrestle the creature to the ground. You throw a net over the beast and carry it down the mountain.

"Here I am," you tell the king's messenger when you arrive in Mycenae once again. "Tell Eurystheus I've brought the Erymanthian boar."

The first labors have been difficult, but you have many labors left to complete. You push forward, all the while thinking of your promise to the gods.

THE END

To follow another path, turn to page 11.

To learn more about Hercules, turn to page 103.

CHAPTER 3

The Augean Stables

When you arrive in Mycenae, King Eurystheus is nowhere to be seen. Someone tells you that he is hiding in a large bronze urn, afraid to face you.

You are the greatest Greek hero. You are not surprised to find that the weak king is afraid of your strength and size. In his place the king's servant tells you the next labor you must complete.

"Your next task," the king's servant says, "is to go to Elis and clean the stables of King Augeas."

Turn the page.

You have defeated vicious beasts and deadly monsters in your labors so far. But now you cannot believe what you are asked to do next. A man of your strength, not to mention a half-god, should never be asked to clean stables. It is beneath you. Even so, you must go. The gods command it.

When you arrive in Elis, you realize this task is much worse than you thought. The stables hold 3,000 cattle, and they have not been cleaned for 30 years.

"You will find this task a difficult one," King Augeas says. You seethe with anger and shame. The king must be joking. "Come," King Augeas says. "At least look at my beautiful cattle."

You reluctantly follow King Augeas along a path near a glittering blue river. Even before you arrive at the stables, the stench nearly makes you sick. The pens in the stone and wood buildings are knee-deep in manure. The cattle wade through their own filth and whine loudly.

"These are the worst stables I have ever seen in my life," you say. "How can you treat your cattle like this?"

"How dare you ..." begins King Augeas, raising his fist. You calmly catch his hand and twist his arm back.

"Calm yourself, King Augeas," you say. "I will do it." But how?

To clean the stables with shovels and brooms,
turn to page 44.

To wash out the stables,
turn to page 46.

You ask King Augeas for his servants to bring you shovels and brooms. "What fun this will be to watch," King Augeas says, laughing.

Soon you begin the task of shoveling out the manure. One by one, stinking piles begin to grow around you. You take up a broom and sweep at the muck. After weeks of work, you still cannot find the stables' stone floors under all the filth. Sweat and dirt coat your face, back, and arms. You look down at your hands holding the broomstick. These hands were made to carry swords and clubs, not brooms. Your anger grows, and you order the servants to fetch King Augeas.

"It took 30 years for these stables to become this dirty," you tell the king as you hand him the broom. "It would take 30 years to clean them."

Your anger has clouded your judgment. You leave Elis without completing your labor. You will not fulfill your promise to the gods. You spend the rest of your days in agony thinking of your family.

THE END

To follow another path, turn to page 11.

To learn more about Hercules, turn to page 103.

You look to the south and see the river Alpheios. To the north flows the river Peneios. The water in each river runs clean and clear. You know what your plan will be.

You set to work digging a trench that stretches all the way to the stables. You dig and dig. The Grecian sun beats down on you. You dig another trench between the two rivers. Your clothes are soaked in sweat. But you do not stop.

When you're finished, the Peneios and the Alpheios rivers flow together. The rivers follow the trench and rush through the stables, carrying with them the piles of manure and filth. The stables sparkle for the first time in years. Pleased with yourself, you kneel at the bank of the newly formed river. The clear water washes the sweat and dirt from your brow.

"You made the rivers do your work!" King Eurystheus roars when you arrive before him in Mycenae. "When you changed the course of the Alpheios and the Peneios rivers, you cheated! You did not accomplish this task!"

You cannot believe what you are hearing. "I was only more clever than you would ever be," you spit out.

"This will not count as one of your labors!" the king says.

Your hand tightens around your club. "You can't do this!" you shout. You are tired and angry.

"That is my decision," the king says as he jumps back into the safety of his urn.

To accept the king's decision,
turn to page 48.

To strike King Eurystheus with your club,
turn to page 52.

You grit your teeth but stay calm. "Very well," you say. The sooner these labors are done, the sooner you will not have to listen to him anymore. "What is my next labor?"

The king pops his head out of the urn and straightens his crooked crown. He pulls at his robes.

"Your next task is to kill the Stymphalian birds in Arcadia," he says.

You laugh. "Kill some birds? I could do that in my sleep!" you say.

"Then let us see you do it," says the king. You laugh again as you set out for Lake Stymphalos.

The heat in Arcadia is intense, and the sun beats down on the land. You begin to sweat inside your armor. As you near the lake, the smells of bird droppings and rotting grasses are strong.

At the water's edge, you see what appear to be human bodies. One bird sits on the shore picking at the bones. With a bow and arrows at your side, you scan the horizon. There are no other people in this place.

Suddenly, great wings rise from one end of the lake. A single bird flies straight toward you. Its razor-sharp beak strikes your armor. You dive to the ground, and the beast flies away. You remove the breastplate and see a hole left by the bird's sharp beak. These are no ordinary birds.

Turn the page.

"Hercules," says a voice behind you. You jump in surprise to see the goddess Athena. "I know Hera and King Eurystheus have sent you on these labors. I am here to help you," she says. "Here is a krotala made by Hephaistos, the god of ironwork. The sound from the krotala will frighten the birds."

Athena hands you the krotala. It is heavy in your palm. You look at Athena in her full armor. The gods are known for tricking mortals. You are not sure you can trust her. How can this rattle help you kill these birds?

To accept Athena's krotala,
turn to page 54.

To refuse Athena's help and use your bow and arrow,
turn to page 60.

"King Eurystheus!" you shout. "That pottery cannot protect you from me." Club in hand, you run toward the urn. You rip the bronze lid off. It falls and rolls around on the ground.

The king, hiding in the pot, looks small and weak. He trembles in fear.

"H … H … Hera will protect me," the king says feebly from inside the urn.

"No one can save you now!" you shout. You raise the club over your head. Just as you are about to bring the club down on King Eurystheus with all your force, you hear a voice.

"You are wrong," says Hera. You freeze as the jealous goddess faces you. It is all the time King Eurystheus' men need to attack and kill you.

THE END

To follow another path, turn to page 11.

To learn more about Hercules, turn to page 103.

You bow your head to the goddess. "Thank you, Athena," you say. "This seems like a strange way to kill birds, but I will try it."

Athena stands back. "You are wise to trust me, Hercules," she says. You take hold of the krotala in one hand. You shake the krotala as hard as you can. The sound is loud enough to wake Hades in the Underworld.

All of a sudden, the birds rise up in confused flocks. They soar up into the sky and fly unevenly. Then they swoop down near you. Only this time they do not try to attack you with their dangerous beaks. One flies in a dizzy circle toward you. You easily grab the bird with your free hand. Breaking its neck, you kill it and drop it in the grass. You catch bird after bird with your hand. Before long Lake Stymphalos is quiet. The man-eating birds are dead.

When you return to Mycenae, King Eurystheus seems surprised to see you.

"You have survived the man-eating birds of Stymphalos?" he asks.

"You didn't think they would destroy me, did you?" you respond.

"Of course not," King Eurystheus says. "And I am glad, because it is my pleasure to give you your next labor—to capture the Cretan bull."

You have heard of the savage bull that roams the island of Crete. It is said that Poseidon, the god of the sea, released the bull on the island as punishment after the Cretan king failed to give the god a sacrifice. The bull has been destroying the land ever since.

Turn the page.

"Bring the bull back here," King Eurystheus says. "My servant will meet you at the city's gates."

The first thing you notice when you arrive on Crete is the miles of broken trees and shrubs of the foothills. A terrifying monster must have caused all this destruction.

Suddenly you hear a snorting, snuffling sound. You jump up just as a great bull comes over a hill. You run after the bull faster than the god Hermes with his winged sandals. Soon you have your strong arms around the bull's thick neck. The giant bull snorts and tries to get out of your grasp. The bull is stronger than you'd expected, but you do not let go. You squeeze harder until you have finally subdued the beast.

Turn the page.

Alarmed by the noise, the people of Crete have crept close. They move around one another to get a closer look at the animal that has plagued their island. They look relieved—and hungry. You are supposed to bring this beast back to King Eurystheus. But imagine how many villagers this animal would feed.

To feast on the bull, go to page 59.

To bring the bull back to Mycenae, turn to page 62.

The people of Crete are struggling. The bull has ravaged their crops and killed all the animals. The people are starving. You plunge your sword into the bull. "We shall feast tonight!" you yell.

That night, you watch the townspeople hungrily feast. They eat like they haven't had a bite of food in years.

"Thank you, Hercules," the people say to you. "You have saved our land and our lives. We will never forget you."

You know that by not bringing the bull back to King Eurystheus, you have not fulfilled your labor. But looking out at the happy people, you decide it was worth it. Even without immortality, you truly are a hero.

THE END

To follow another path, turn to page 11.

To learn more about Hercules, turn to page 103.

"Thank you, Athena," you say with a laugh, "but I do not need a child's toy to help me. Save your rattle for a musician."

"You are a fool, Hercules," Athena says, taking back the krotala and hiding it in the folds of her robe. As she turns and walks away, you look across the lake. You see one lonely bird rising up. You take aim with your bow. The arrow flies true but only grazes the bird's wing. A single blue-grey feather falls right at you.

The last thing you hear is Athena's voice. "You will never kill those birds now," she says, as the bird's razor-sharp feather pierces your heart.

THE END

To follow another path, turn to page 11.

To learn more about Hercules, turn to page 103.

No, you think to yourself. *I have a job to do. I must bring this bull back to Mycenae.*

You grab the bull's horns and mount the beast. The bull snorts in anger. It bucks and kicks as it tries to knock you to the ground. You hold on as tightly as you can. You have learned to ride the wildest beasts. Your balance is unshakeable.

"King Eurystheus will have his bull," you shout as you ride the Cretan bull toward the island's shore.

When you return to Mycenae, the king's servant meets you at the city's gates. You let the bull run loose in Eurystheus' pastures.

"Your next labor, Hercules," says the servant, "is to bring back the four mares of Diomedes."

"How many beasts does King Eurystheus want in his kingdom?" you ask, shaking your head. Without waiting for an answer, you begin your journey to Thrace. You have heard this is where you will find the mares.

You arrive in Thrace after several days' travel by chariot. The sun is just rising as you stand atop a hillside. In the pasture below, you see the four mares. They are beautiful horses. Their sleek brown coats glisten in the sunlight. They paw at the ground and stamp their hooves. A soft breeze carries the sound of their whinnies.

Turn the page.

As you watch, a servant of Diomedes walks briskly into the pasture. Instantly the mood changes. You see the four horses surround the servant. They snort and stamp. In an instant they charge wildly, knocking the servant to the ground. They tear at the man's flesh with ironlike teeth. He screams for help, but it is over before you can run to his aid. This will be harder than you thought.

To try to tame the horses,
turn to page 66.

To try to fight the horses,
turn to page 68.

You stand a good distance from the horses. They are dangerous, but you have tamed many horses in your time. The key is to get them to trust you. You put down your sword and club and slowly creep toward the mares.

"Calm," you say in a soothing voice. "Come to Hercules." The horses whinny and stamp, but they do not charge.

With no weapons and no fear, you slowly approach the horses. You have come prepared, with a rope tied around your waist. One by one you tie each horse. They breathe smoke but do not attack. When you have them all tied, you hitch them to your chariot. They look magnificent. Driving the four mares away from Thrace is easy now that they are tamed. You continue to speak gently and quietly to them. The horses are calm during the journey to Mycenae.

But as soon as you arrive at the king's palace, all four horses begin to buck and kick. The king's servants are wide-eyed as you lead the angry beasts to the palace.

"Here are the horses," you say to a servant. "I will leave them in his stables. Tell King Eurystheus I have completed this labor."

Once in the stables, the horses stamp their hooves and paw at the pen. The servants tremble with fear.

"Be careful when you feed them," you say with a wink.

With even more confidence, you are ready to tackle the rest of the labors put before you.

THE END

To follow another path, turn to page 11.

To learn more about Hercules, turn to page 103.

Arming yourself with your club and sword, you start down the hill toward the horses. Smoke rises from their noses as they sniffle and neigh.

You are close enough to the four mares now to feel the heat rising off their sleek flanks. All but one is turned away from you. You raise your club in one hand and your sword in the other. Suddenly the one watching you rises onto its back legs. The other three turn to face you. Their eyes are blood red and their teeth are yellow. You have no choice but to fight.

You launch yourself toward them. You hit one with your club. You feel your sword make contact with another. But a third has your foot in its mouth. You swing your club just as the fourth knocks it from your hand.

The moment your foot is released, you turn to run back up the hill. But the four horses stampede at your heels. Before you know what is happening, all four are tearing at your flesh. Even you are no match for them.

THE END

To follow another path, turn to page 11.

To learn more about Hercules, turn to page 103.

CHAPTER 4

The Amazon Queen

With eight labors already completed, you start to believe you can finish King Eurytheus' impossible tasks. You approach him in his palace, ready for your ninth labor.

"You are a strong man, Hercules," King Eurystheus says. "But can you face the Amazon warriors?"

"I'm not afraid of any of your tasks," you say.

"Let me be the judge of that," says the king. "Your labor is to bring me the belt of Hippolyte, queen of the Amazons."

Turn the page.

The Amazons are a band of fierce women who live in Themiscyra. They are strong warriors with sharp weapons. The Amazons protect their lands and battle their enemies. Bringing back the belt of Hippolyte may be your most difficult labor yet.

After a long journey across the sea, you arrive where the Amazons live. The women are on horseback and wear armor. They carry their swords at the ready.

"Which one of you is Hippolyte, queen of the Amazons?" you ask the warriors who stand before you.

One of the Amazons steps forward. She is taller than you and almost as broad. Her muscles are thick and her eyes are dangerous.

"I am Hippolyte," says the queen. "And who are you?" Around her waist is a belt of strong leather and gold.

"I am Hercules, the son of Zeus," you say.

You request to speak to the queen in private, away from the other Amazons. "I have come for your belt, Hippolyte," you say when you are alone.

"My belt? Do you know that this belt was given to me by Ares, the god of war?" she asks. You can see her fist tighten around her sword. "Ares gave me this belt because I am the best warrior of all the Amazons."

To fight Hippolyte for her belt,
turn to page 74.

To reason with Hippolyte,
turn to page 78.

You look more closely at the queen. She may be a skilled warrior, but can she beat you?

"Give me the belt," you say as you draw your sword. "Or I will have to kill you."

"You will have to fight me for it, young man," Hippolyte says. At this, she raises her sword. But you are just as fast. The two swords clash, the sound ringing out across the land.

"It's just a belt, Hippolyte," you say. "Why not give it to me?"

Hippolyte lunges toward you and barely misses your left side. You lunge forward and the swords clash once again.

"Every man who has come to see the Amazons has stayed," she says with a smile, "as a slave." As she speaks, you grab hold of her arm. Her sword falls to the ground.

"And now," you say through gritted teeth, "give me the belt or I will kill you."

"Let me go, Hercules," she says. "I will consider giving you my belt." The Amazon queen's eyes look honest.

Hippolyte agrees to give you her belt for your labor. But the goddess Hera has other plans. Disguised as an Amazon warrior, Hera warns each of the Amazons that you plan to kidnap their queen. As you turn to leave with Hippolyte's belt, you see the other Amazons have surrounded you. Each warrior has her sword raised.

"Was this a trap?" you ask the Amazon queen. You spin around behind Hippolyte and hold your sword across her neck.

Turn the page.

"Stay back," you say to the other Amazons, "or I will kill your queen!" The Amazons do not lower their swords.

You kill Hippolyte with your sword and quickly strap the golden belt around your waist. You narrowly escape the other Amazons and set sail on your ship. With the belt in your hands, you set sail for Mycenae.

King Eurystheus' servant takes the Amazon's belt and tells you of your next labor. You must bring back the cattle owned by the three-bodied monster Geryon. You are exhausted from your labors. But the sooner you go, the sooner you will be done with King Eurystheus and his tasks.

You set sail for the Inner Sea in a large ship heading west. The sea is calm, but the sun shines brightly. As the day continues, you get a headache from squinting into the sun's rays.

"I will never make it west with this hot sun!" you say. "I will shoot the sun out of the sky so that it does not get in my eyes!"

You set an arrow into your bow. Just then you hear a voice. "Hercules," the voice says. "I am Helios, god of the sun."

"So you are the one who put this ball of fire in the sky," you say angrily as you point your bow up to the sky.

"Put down your bow, Hercules," Helios commands. "Shooting the sun will not help you."

To ignore Helios and shoot the sun,
turn to page 80.

To listen to Helios,
turn to page 82.

"Hippolyte, your majesty," you say. "I could fight you for the belt. But neither of us wants to die today."

"That is true," she agrees with an evil smile.

"I need your belt to bring to King Eurystheus. I have been given 12 labors to complete for the gods of Mount Olympus," you explain.

"You will never succeed," Hippolyte laughs.

You realize that as you have been talking, the other Amazons have reappeared and are now surrounding you. You can feel their breath on the back of your neck. You look behind you to see that each of them has raised a sword.

Suddenly, the warriors lunge toward you. Steel blades flash. You grab for your own sword but discover someone has removed it. In one swift move, Hippolyte has her sword at your throat.

"Don't you agree," Hippolyte says to the women gathered around her, "that Hercules must be taught a lesson?" The Amazons laugh with Hippolyte as she kills you.

THE END

To follow another path, turn to page 11.

To learn more about Hercules, turn to page 103.

You don't listen to Helios. You are angry. You slowly pull back the bowstring, stretching the sinew tight to test its strength. You fit an arrow into the bow. Its point is sharp and ready.

"I have labors to complete, Helios. And your sun is in my way," you say. You take aim and shoot. Suddenly the world is plunged into darkness. It is so dark, you cannot see the deck of the ship. You cannot even see your mighty hand in front of your face.

"Hercules," you hear Helios say in a mighty voice. "What have you done? The world will have no light, no food, no hunting."

In the darkness, you realize your quest is over. You slowly starve to death knowing you failed.

THE END

To follow another path, turn to page 11.

To learn more about Hercules, turn to page 103.

Your hands are wet with sweat. You lower the arrow.

"Very well, Helios," you say. "I will not shoot the sun. But I still have a task to perform for King Eurystheus. I must travel to where the monster Geryon lives. How can I do this with the sun in my eyes?"

"You have chosen wisely," Helios says. "I will reward you."

Suddenly the light is even brighter as a huge golden vessel appears beside your ship.

"This is my ship," Helios says. "You may travel in it. There is no need to steer or navigate because this is a magic ship. It will take you wherever you need to go."

You stare at the ship as it sparkles in the brilliant light of the sun.

"Thank you, Helios," you say. "With this magic vessel, I will make it to the far west." On the new golden ship, you continue the journey westward. Swiftly and easily, you cross the sea. The sun rises and sets many times before your journey is over, but it never shines as strong or hot.

At last you come to the land where the monster Geryon lives. Herds of his red cattle graze quietly on pastureland. These beasts will be easy to bring back to Mycenae. You see no sign of the monster Geryon.

Turn the page.

Then you hear a roar. You turn to see a giant with three bodies joined to one pair of legs. Its three terrible mouths gape open, exposing sharp teeth and black tongues.

"Argh!" roars Geryon. He begins to rush toward you, his three bodies working as one. You have to think quickly.

You load an arrow into your bow and fire at the beast. It pierces one of his bodies. Quickly you load another arrow. It strikes the monster's second body. The third arrow flies into the remaining body. The three bodies of Geryon stumble and fall. Your arrows have killed the monster. You herd the cattle to the shore and load them into Helios' ship.

Turn the page.

When you return to Mycenae, you release the cattle to graze in the hilly pasture. The king says your next labor is to bring back the Golden Apples of the Hesperides. The Hesperides are the three lovely daughters of the god Atlas.

Compared to killing beasts and tracking wild animals, you think this will be an easy task. You know that Atlas stands in the west, holding up the heavens. So again you travel west, this time to North Africa.

When you land on the shores, a soft breeze carries a sugary scent of honey and perfume. You follow the scent. Soon you find yourself in a hidden and secret garden. The trees are lush and green. The flowers are sweet. In the middle of the garden, you see an apple tree with branches heavy with golden apples.

As you approach the tree, you hear a low grumble. At the tree's base is a dragon wrapped around the trunk. The dragon growls again, its green scales shimmering. The dragon bares its teeth. It is only a small dragon, but the sound coming from the animal is fierce. The apples glitter and shine. You extend your arm to pick an apple, but before you can pluck the golden fruit, you hear voices.

"Be careful!" You turn to see three lovely girls in long flowing robes.

"You must be the Hesperides," you say. "I have come to collect the golden apples."

"The dragon will not let you pick them," they warn. "It will surely kill you."

To pick the apples, turn to page 89.

To listen to the Hesperides' warning, turn to page 90.

You look at the apples shining on the tree. You could easily reach out and take one. Down below, the dragon's scales glisten as it curls itself tightly around the tree's trunk. You can see its sharp claws dig into the bark.

You think of all the labors you have completed so far. Then you think of your wife and children.

"I must pick these apples," you say.

With one last glance at the dragon, you take hold of an apple and turn to run. But even before you hear the dragon's roar, the Hesperides scream. The dragon is surprisingly fast. You cry out as the dragon's teeth sinks into your flesh. As you lay dying, the apple falls from your grasp and rolls along the ground.

THE END

To follow another path, turn to page 11.

To learn more about Hercules, turn to page 103.

As you look at the glistening fruit on the tree, you see something out of the corner of your eye. Standing just beyond the tree you see the Hesperides' father, Atlas. You recognize him by the sky on his shoulders. He stands at a crouch, his knees bent from the weight of the heavens. He looks tired. That gives you an idea.

"I need your help, Atlas," you say.

"Can't you see that I am busy?" Atlas grumbles. "I must hold the sky on my shoulders forever. I am tired. I cannot help you."

To trick Atlas into helping you,
go to page 91.

To demand that Atlas help you,
turn to page 96.

"I see that you are tired, Atlas," you say to him. "Holding up the heavens must be a very tough job indeed." Atlas sadly nods his head.

"I am Hercules, son of a god. If you will pick the golden apples for me," you continue, "I will hold up the sky for you. This will give you a rest."

Atlas considers for a moment. "It would be good to put down this burden," he says. He hands you the heavens, which you set upon your own strong shoulders. Rubbing his back, Atlas goes to the tree. He easily plucks three apples from its branches. The dragon doesn't stir.

"I have picked your apples," says Atlas. "But it feels good to let go of my burden. I do not think I want to hold it up any longer."

Turn the page.

You must think fast. You cannot stay here holding Atlas' burden. You must return to Mycenae with the apples.

"I will gladly hold the sky, Atlas," you say. "But it hurts my shoulders. If you will just hold it for a moment while I get a cushion, I will take over your job."

"Thank you, Hercules," says Atlas, taking back his burden. As soon as the sky is resting firmly on Atlas' shoulders again, you grab the golden apples.

"I'm sorry, Atlas," you yell as you run away from the garden of the Hesperides. "Holding the heavens is your job, not mine."

Atlas roars and shakes the heavens in anger, but there is nothing he can do. You sail back to King Eurystheus to fulfill your labor.

King Eurystheus takes the golden apples from you and returns them to the Hesperides.

"For your final task," he says, "you must bring back Cerberus."

"But Cerberus guards the gates of the Underworld!" you protest.

"Yes, that is correct," says the king with a sneer. "You must bring the dog back to me, if you can survive."

The Underworld is ruled by the god Hades. Only the dead can go to the Underworld, and no one returns. You know this will be your most challenging task yet.

Turn the page.

Reluctantly you ask Hades to be allowed to enter the Underworld and leave again. Hades will let you pass, but only if you do not use weapons to complete your labor. You agree.

When you arrive, you find the Underworld is even more terrible than you imagined. It is hot with burning fires. Winged ghosts with snakes for hair fly past you.

At last you see Cerberus. It is no ordinary dog. It has three heads, each with teeth more vicious than the other. Its mouths drool, and its jaws snap. Its eyes are red coals. Its tail is like a dragon's. Snakeheads come out of its back. You have never seen anything more frightening in your life.

Cerberus begins to growl. It makes a low, rumbling noise. The very Earth seems to shake at the sound. The hairs on the back of your neck stand on end. You regret agreeing to Hades' demands. How can this creature be captured without a weapon?

To try to capture Cerberus with your bare hands,
turn to page 98.

To break your promise to Hades
and use a weapon to fight Cerberus,
turn to page 101.

"You will do as I say," you tell Atlas. "I am the strongest man in the world."

"That may be, but I cannot help you," says Atlas sadly.

"But I am the son of Zeus, the ruler of all the gods. Think of what I could do to you!" you shout. You stand nose to nose with Atlas. But Atlas only shakes his head.

"You must pick the apples for me!" you demand. You are furious now. "I need them to complete my labors. If you don't, I'll kill you with my bare hands."

"You may be the strongest man," says Atlas. "But I am the one holding up the sky."

He laughs bitterly. On hearing his laugh, you can no longer stop yourself. You beat him with your fists. With one last mighty blow, you kill him. Atlas drops his burden. As the skies fall, you and the rest of the world die.

THE END

To follow another path, turn to page 11.

To learn more about Hercules, turn to page 103.

You look at the dog, which growls at you. Its massive shoulders are bigger than yours. Its red eyes glare at you.

"I promised Hades I would not use a weapon," you remind yourself.

The horrible beast barks and snarls. It grabs hold of your arm with an iron grip. You manage to shake yourself loose. Your hands form iron fists. You stun two of its heads in one blow. One more punch, and the dog falls the to floor. The beast is out cold.

Hades allows you to carry Cerberus out of the Underworld. The three mouths leave a trail of drool as you carry it back to the land of the living.

You present Cerberus to King Eurystheus. He is already hiding in his urn.

"King Eurystheus," you say. "Come out!"

Turn the page.

The king pops his head out of the urn. "Get that creature back to Hades!" he commands. You laugh as the king trembles with fear.

"I have finished my 12 labors," you say. You are no longer laughing. It has been a long journey and you are ready for it to be over. Cerberus wakes up and starts to growl.

"Send that dog away!" the king squeals.

"Very well," you reply. "Now that you have seen that I have completed this task, I will return Cerberus to the Underworld."

Cerberus once again guards the Underworld, and you have completed all your labors. The gods have forgiven you for the death of your family, and you are granted immortality.

THE END

To follow another path, turn to page 11.

To learn more about Hercules, turn to page 103.

Your fingers close on the handle of your dagger. "Even though I promised Hades I would do this without a weapon, there is no other way," you say.

You point the blade at the beast's heart. But as you move to strike, the dog's sharp teeth rip into your flesh. You try again, but the dog's dragon tail trips you.

You fall and the beast's teeth are at your throat. It holds you down with sharp claws. You stare into the red eyes of Cerberus, wishing you had never come into the Underworld. You will never complete this task. And you will never leave the Underworld alive.

THE END

To follow another path, turn to page 11.

To learn more about Hercules, turn to page 103.

CHAPTER 5

Immortality

Hercules is one of the most well-known figures in Greek mythology. Because he is only half-god, his incredible strength is even more amazing. Hercules looks like a man but has the strength of 20 men. His heroic feats and accomplishments were the subject of many stories told by ancient Greeks.

Even before completing the 12 labors, Hercules traveled many lands and fought many wars, always using his incredible strength to beat opponents. In one adventure, Hercules joined his father Zeus to battle two huge giants who threw boulders at Mount Olympus. Zeus struck the giants with his thunderbolt, but it is Hercules who defeated them.

Turn the page.

Hercules was a hero, but he also had a quick temper and would fight anyone who upset him. When Hercules learned to play the lyre, he became frustrated and struck his music teacher. The teacher died from Hercules' strong blow.

Despite this, many of his adventures made Hercules a hero. He made close friends and rescued maidens. When the wife of his friend King Admetus died, Hercules went back to the Underworld to find her. With his great strength, Hercules fought Death and brought King Admetus' wife back to the land of the living.

When Hercules returned from his 12 labors, he married a beautiful woman named Deianira. But Deianira was a jealous woman. She asked a centaur, a creature that is half man and half horse, for a love potion.

When Deianira used the potion on Hercules, she found that it was actually a deadly poison. Despite being poisoned, Hercules did not die, because of the immortality he earned after he accomplished his 12 labors. Instead Hercules was taken to Mount Olympus to live with his father, Zeus. There he made peace with Hera at last. Hercules eventually married Hera's daughter, the goddess Hebe. He lives with Hebe like one of the gods for eternity.

Greek Gods and Goddesses

Apollo—god of many things, including music, archery, light, and knowledge. Healing and medicine are often associated with Apollo. Zeus is Artemis' father, and Artemis is his sister.

Ares—god of war and courage. Ares and Zeus are brothers.

Athena—goddess of wisdom and protector of heroes. She was one of the ancient Greek's most important gods, as they valued wisdom above all else. In many Greek myths, Athena provided heroes with help to succeed on their quests. Athena was Zeus' daughter.

Artemis—goddess of the hunt. Artemis protected animals and nature, including the Cerynean stag. Zeus is Artemis' father.

Atlas—one of the 12 original Greek gods, known as Titans. As a Titan, Atlas waged war against Zeus and his set of gods, known as the Olympians. Atlas and the other Titans lost the war. Zeus forced Atlas to stand on the edge of Earth and hold up the sky until the end of time.

Hades—god of the dead, who rules the Underworld. Zeus and Hades are brothers.

Hebe—goddess of youth and Hera's daughter. Hebe married Hercules when he came to live on Mount Olympus.

Helios—god of the sun. Helios drove the golden sun chariot across the sky everyday to raise the sun. Four winged horses pulled his chariot.

Hera—queen of the gods and goddess of marriage. She was married to Zeus. Hera was a jealous wife, as Zeus had many children with other goddesses and mortal women. Hera often thwarted Greek heroes who were Zeus' sons.

Zeus—god of the sky and ruler of the Greek gods. Zeus was also the father of many of the most famous Greek heroes, such as Hercules and Perseus. His weapon was a thunderbolt.

OTHER PATHS TO EXPLORE

In this book, you've experienced the 12 labors of Hercules the hero, but the story isn't over. Here are some other Greek myths that share characters with the stories you just read.

1. Hercules joins Jason and his crew of 50 heroes, called the Argonauts, on the search for the Golden Fleece. However, Hercules abandons Jason and the rest of the crew in the middle of the journey. Jason battled harpies and sea monsters. How do you think Hercules could have helped if he had stayed with Jason? (Integration of Knowledge and Ideas)

2. The 12 labors begin because Hera hated Hercules so much. Her hatred was so strong, she tricked Hercules into killing his wife Magara and their sons. When Hercules realizes what he has done, he is horrified. How would the stories of Hercules have been different if Hera didn't hate him? (Integration of Knowledge and Ideas)

3. When Hercules visited his friend King Admetus, he finds that the king's wife has died. Hercules travels to the Underworld to rescue the queen. Hercules had been to the Underworld before during his 12 labors. Do you think Hercules would have offered to rescue the king's wife if he hadn't been to the Underworld before? Why or why not? (Integration of Knowledge and Ideas)

Hoena, Blake. *The 12 Labors of Hercules: A Graphic Retelling.* Ancient Myths. North Mankato, Minn.: Capstone Press, 2015.

Powell, Martin. *The Adventures of Hercules: A Graphic Novel. Graphic Revolve.* North Mankato, Minn.: Stone Arch Books, 2014.

Van Lente, Fred. *Hercules.* Heroes and Legends. New York: Rosen Publishing, 2015.

INTERNET SITES

FactHound offers a safe, fun way to find Internet sites related to this book. All of the sites on FactHound have been researched by our staff.

Here's all you do:
Visit *www.facthound.com*
Type in this code: 9781491481110

chariot (CHAYR-ee-uht)—a small vehicle pulled by a horse; chariots were used in ancient times for battles and racing

hide (HYDE)—an animal's skin

immortal (i-MOR-tuhl)—able to live forever

lyre (LIRE)—a small, stringed harplike instrument played mostly in ancient Egypt, Israel, and Greece

manure (muh-NOO-ur)—animal waste

mortal (MOR-tuhl)—human, referring to a being who will eventually die

seethe (SEETH)—to be very angry or excited

sinew (SIN-yoo)—a strong fiber or band of tissue that connects a muscle to a bone

stag (STAG)—an adult male deer

Underworld (UHN-dur-wurld)—the place under the earth where the spirits of the dead go according to ancient Greek, Roman, and Egyptian beliefs

vessel (VESS-uhl)—a ship or a large boat

British Museum. (n.d.). *Ancient Greece.* http://www.ancientgreece.co.uk/menu.html

Buxton, R. (2004). *The Complete World of Greek Mythology.* London: Thames & Hudson.

Davis, K. C. (2005). *Don't Know Much About Mythology.* New York: HarperCollins.

Essential Visual History of World Mythology. (2008). Washington, DC: National Geographic.

Evslin, B. (1975). *God, Demigods & Demons: An Encyclopedia of Greek Mythology.* New York: Scholastic.

Frazer, J. G., Trans. (1979). *Apollodorus: The Library, Vol. II: Book 3.10–16.* Cambridge, MA: Loeb Classical Library.

Scott, M. (2009, November). *The Rise of Women in Ancient Greece. History Today.*

Tufts University. Classics Department. Perseus Project. (2008). Hercules: Greece's Greatest Hero. http://www.perseus.tufts.edu/Herakles/index.html

Vellacott, P., Trans. (1963). *Euripides: Medea and Other Plays.* London: Penguin.

Waterfield, R., Trans. (2003). *Euripides: Children of Heracles, Hippolytus, Adromache, Hecuba.* New York: Oxford.

Wilkinson, P. (1998). *Illustrated Dictionary of Mythology.* London: DK.